MAD LIBS®

HAPPY NEW YEAR
MAD LIBS

by Gabrielle Reyes

MAD LIBS

An Imprint of Penguin Random House LLC, New York

Mad Libs format and text copyright © 2019 by Penguin Random House LLC. All rights reserved.

Concept created by Roger Price & Leonard Stern

Cover illustration by Scott Brooks

Published by Mad Libs,
an imprint of Penguin Random House LLC, New York.
Printed in the USA.

Visit us online at www.penguinrandomhouse.com.

ISBN 9780593092996
3 5 7 9 10 8 6 4

INSTRUCTIONS

MAD LIBS® is a game for people who don't like games!
It can be played by one, two, three, four, or forty.

• RIDICULOUSLY SIMPLE DIRECTIONS

In this tablet you will find stories containing blank spaces where words
are left out. One player, the READER, selects one of these stories. The
READER does not tell anyone what the story is about. Instead, he/she asks
the other players, the WRITERS, to give him/her words. These words are
used to fill in the blank spaces in the story.

• TO PLAY

The READER asks each WRITER in turn to call out a word—an adjective or
a noun or whatever the space calls for—and uses them to fill in the blank
spaces in the story. The result is a MAD LIBS® game.

When the READER then reads the completed MAD LIBS® game to the other
players, they will discover that they have written a story that is fantastic,
screamingly funny, shocking, silly, crazy, or just plain dumb—depending
upon which words each WRITER called out.

• EXAMPLE (*Before* and *After*)

" _____ !" he said _____
          EXCLAMATION   ADVERB

as he jumped into his convertible _____ and
                                              NOUN

drove off with his _____ wife.
                              ADJECTIVE

" _____**OUCH**_____ !" he said _____**HAPPILY**_____
          EXCLAMATION   ADVERB

as he jumped into his convertible _____**CAT**_____ and
                                              NOUN

drove off with his _____**BRAVE**_____ wife.
                              ADJECTIVE

In case you have forgotten what adjectives, adverbs, nouns, and verbs are, here is a quick review:

An **ADJECTIVE** describes something or somebody. *Lumpy, soft, ugly, messy,* and *short* are adjectives.

An **ADVERB** tells how something is done. It modifies a verb and usually ends in "ly." *Modestly, stupidly, greedily,* and *carefully* are adverbs.

A **NOUN** is the name of a person, place, or thing. *Sidewalk, umbrella, bridle, bathtub,* and *nose* are nouns.

A **VERB** is an action word. *Run, pitch, jump,* and *swim* are verbs. Put the verbs in past tense if the directions say PAST TENSE. *Ran, pitched, jumped,* and *swam* are verbs in the past tense.

When we ask for **A PLACE**, we mean any sort of place: a country or city (*Spain, Cleveland*) or a room (*bathroom, kitchen*).

An **EXCLAMATION** or **SILLY WORD** is any sort of funny sound, gasp, grunt, or outcry, like *Wow!, Ouch!, Whomp!, Ick!,* and *Gadzooks!*

When we ask for specific words, like a **NUMBER**, a **COLOR**, an **ANIMAL**, or a **PART OF THE BODY**, we mean a word that is one of those things, like *seven, blue, horse,* or *head*.

When we ask for a **PLURAL**, it means more than one. For example, *cat* pluralized is *cats*.

MAD LIBS® is fun to play with friends, but you can also play it by yourself! To begin with, DO NOT look at the story on the page below. Fill in the blanks on this page with the words called for. Then, using the words you have selected, fill in the blank spaces in the story.

Now you've created your own hilarious MAD LIBS® game!

THROW THE CONFETTI

ADJECTIVE _____

COLOR _____

TYPE OF LIQUID _____

ARTICLE OF CLOTHING (PLURAL) _____

ADJECTIVE _____

ADJECTIVE _____

ANIMAL _____

PERSON IN ROOM _____

NOUN _____

ADJECTIVE _____

PART OF THE BODY (PLURAL) _____

ANIMAL _____

VERB ENDING IN "ING" _____

OCCUPATION _____

PART OF THE BODY _____

SAME PART OF THE BODY _____

VERB _____

MAD LIBS®

THROW THE CONFETTI

Try one of these _____ party themes to make New Year's Eve
                        ADJECTIVE

a night to remember:

Glitter and Gold: Host a/an _____ -tie event. String the
                                      COLOR

lights and pop the _____ ! Have everyone wear their
                         TYPE OF LIQUID

fanciest _____ . New Year's Eve is the
              ARTICLE OF CLOTHING (PLURAL)

_____ time to sparkle and shine.
   ADJECTIVE

Murder Mystery: What happens in the new year is unknown—and so

is the killer at your _____ mystery night! Solve the case of the
                            ADJECTIVE

missing _____ , or figure out who stole _____ 's
              ANIMAL   PERSON IN ROOM

treasured _____ .
                NOUN

Dance Party: All you need is a/an _____ playlist to get your
                                              ADJECTIVE

guests on their _____ . Break out the newest dance
                      PART OF THE BODY (PLURAL)

moves, like the Funky _____ and the _____
                              ANIMAL   VERB ENDING IN "ING"

_____ .
      OCCUPATION

Game Night: Go _____ to _____ in an
                          PART OF THE BODY   SAME PART OF THE BODY

all-night board game challenge. Who will _____ the title
                                                    VERB

of "New Year's Champion"?

MAD LIBS® is fun to play with friends, but you can also play it by yourself! To begin with, DO NOT look at the story on the page below. Fill in the blanks on this page with the words called for. Then, using the words you have selected, fill in the blank spaces in the story.

Now you've created your own hilarious MAD LIBS® game!

YOU'RE INVITED!

ADJECTIVE _____

A PLACE _____

PERSON IN ROOM _____

NOUN _____

NOUN _____

TYPE OF LIQUID _____

TYPE OF FOOD (PLURAL) _____

PART OF THE BODY _____

PLURAL NOUN _____

ARTICLE OF CLOTHING (PLURAL) _____

CELEBRITY _____

PERSON IN ROOM _____

NOUN _____

ARTICLE OF CLOTHING (PLURAL) _____

YOU'RE INVITED!

Join us for the most _____ party of the century this
                        ADJECTIVE

New Year's Eve at (the) _____. The party is hosted
                          A PLACE

by _____, and the theme is _____
    PERSON IN ROOM   NOUN

and _____.
        NOUN

We'll have:

• A/An _____ fountain with _____
          TYPE OF LIQUID   TYPE OF FOOD (PLURAL)

  for dipping

• _____ painting and glitter tattoos
    PART OF THE BODY

• A photo booth with a whole bunch of _____ and
                                          PLURAL NOUN

_____ to wear
ARTICLE OF CLOTHING (PLURAL)

But that's not all! Just after midnight, _____ will be
                                              CELEBRITY

performing for the first time ever with _____. Don't
                                            PERSON IN ROOM

miss this once-in-a-lifetime _____. Wear your dancing
                                  NOUN

_____, and let's end this year in style.
ARTICLE OF CLOTHING (PLURAL)

MAD LIBS® is fun to play with friends, but you can also play it by yourself! To begin with, DO NOT look at the story on the page below. Fill in the blanks on this page with the words called for. Then, using the words you have selected, fill in the blank spaces in the story.

Now you've created your own hilarious MAD LIBS® game!

MY SPECIAL NEW YEAR'S EVE TRADITIONS

EXCLAMATION _____

NOUN _____

ADJECTIVE _____

ARTICLE OF CLOTHING _____

PLURAL NOUN _____

PLURAL NOUN _____

NUMBER _____

NOUN _____

PLURAL NOUN _____

ADJECTIVE _____

TYPE OF FOOD (PLURAL) _____

ADVERB _____

ADJECTIVE _____

SILLY WORD _____

PART OF THE BODY (PLURAL) _____

ADJECTIVE _____

MAD LIBS®
MY SPECIAL NEW YEAR'S EVE TRADITIONS

_____! New Year's _____ is almost here! This
　　EXCLAMATION　　　　　　　　　　　　　NOUN

year, I'm creating my own New Year's Eve traditions. They're going to

be super _____ . First, I'll wear a sparkly _____
　　　　　　ADJECTIVE　　　　　　　　　　　　　ARTICLE OF CLOTHING

with _____ all over it. Then, with my family and
　　　　PLURAL NOUN

_____ , we'll start the countdown at _____ seconds
　　PLURAL NOUN　　　　　　　　　　　　　　　　　　　NUMBER

to midnight. As soon as the _____ strikes twelve, we'll make
　　　　　　　　　　　　　　　　　NOUN

some noise! We'll grab _____ and shake them like crazy
　　　　　　　　　　　　PLURAL NOUN

while _____ fireworks light up the night sky. Next, we'll eat
　　　ADJECTIVE

twelve _____ as _____ as we can. That's
　　　　TYPE OF FOOD (PLURAL)　　　　ADVERB

one for each month of the year. This will give us _____ luck
　　　　　　　　　　　　　　　　　　　　　　　　　ADJECTIVE

all year long. Finally, we'll say "_____" while shaking our
　　　　　　　　　　　　　　　　　SILLY WORD

_____ to get a/an _____ start to the
　　PART OF THE BODY (PLURAL)　　　　　　ADJECTIVE

new year.

MAD LIBS® is fun to play with friends, but you can also play it by yourself! To begin with, DO NOT look at the story on the page below. Fill in the blanks on this page with the words called for. Then, using the words you have selected, fill in the blank spaces in the story.

Now you've created your own hilarious MAD LIBS® game!

NO NEW YEAR'S PLANS?
NO PROBLEM!

PART OF THE BODY _____

ADJECTIVE _____

ADJECTIVE _____

NOUN _____

ADJECTIVE _____

ADJECTIVE _____

VEHICLE _____

NUMBER _____

ADJECTIVE _____

TYPE OF FOOD _____

PART OF THE BODY _____

NOUN _____

ADJECTIVE _____

NUMBER _____

ADJECTIVE _____

TYPE OF FOOD _____

OCCUPATION _____

MAD LIBS
NO NEW YEAR'S PLANS?
NO PROBLEM!

Start your new year on the right _____ with these
PART OF THE BODY

_____ New Year's Day activities.
ADJECTIVE

- **New Year, New Superhero:** The world needs a/an _____
  ADJECTIVE

  superhero that *you* create! What superpowers would your

  _____ have? Make a/an _____ costume, invent
  NOUN   ADJECTIVE

  a/an _____ identity, and design your getaway
       ADJECTIVE

  _____. Then you'll be all set to save the day—and the
  VEHICLE

  year ahead.

- **Try Something New:** Make a list of _____ new things to
  NUMBER

  try this year. Eat new foods, like _____ shrimp or fried
                                       ADJECTIVE

  _____. Play new sports, like _____-ball or
  TYPE OF FOOD   PART OF THE BODY

  _____ tennis.
  NOUN

- **Cooking Competition:** Grab your _____ friend and set
                                       ADJECTIVE

  up a cook-off. In _____ minutes or less, make the most
                    NUMBER

  _____ dish you can using _____. Whoever wins
  ADJECTIVE   TYPE OF FOOD

  becomes "Top _____ of the New Year."
               OCCUPATION

MAD LIBS® is fun to play with friends, but you can also play it by yourself! To begin with, DO NOT look at the story on the page below. Fill in the blanks on this page with the words called for. Then, using the words you have selected, fill in the blank spaces in the story.

Now you've created your own hilarious MAD LIBS® game!

FASHION FORWARD

ADJECTIVE _____

VERB _____

COLOR _____

ARTICLE OF CLOTHING (PLURAL) _____

ADJECTIVE _____

PART OF THE BODY _____

CELEBRITY _____

NOUN _____

ARTICLE OF CLOTHING (PLURAL) _____

SILLY WORD _____

PART OF THE BODY _____

ARTICLE OF CLOTHING (PLURAL) _____

VERB _____

ADJECTIVE _____

COLOR _____

ADJECTIVE _____

VERB ENDING IN "ING" _____

PART OF THE BODY _____

MAD LIBS®

FASHION FORWARD

Kid 1: The new year is the _____ time to try new looks. I'm
ADJECTIVE

going to _____ all kinds of fashion this year. How about you?
VERB

Kid 2: Definitely. I'm going to start by wearing _____
COLOR

_____ with _____ buttons. I'm also
ARTICLE OF CLOTHING (PLURAL)   ADJECTIVE

going to wear more accessories on my _____ this year,
PART OF THE BODY

like _____ .
CELEBRITY

Kid 1: "Go big or go _____" is my catchphrase for the
NOUN

new year. I want to wear _____ that shout
ARTICLE OF CLOTHING (PLURAL)

"_____!"
SILLY WORD

Kid 2: What should I wear for _____-ball practice?
PART OF THE BODY

I need comfortable _____ so I can run and
ARTICLE OF CLOTHING (PLURAL)

_____ .
VERB

Kid 1: How about a/an _____-sleeved shirt and shorts with
ADJECTIVE

_____ sneakers?
COLOR

Kid 2: Sounds like a/an _____ plan.
ADJECTIVE

Kid 1: _____ our own styles is so fun! We'll look
VERB ENDING IN "ING"

amazing from head to _____ .
PART OF THE BODY

MAD LIBS® is fun to play with friends, but you can also play it by yourself! To begin with, DO NOT look at the story on the page below. Fill in the blanks on this page with the words called for. Then, using the words you have selected, fill in the blank spaces in the story.

Now you've created your own hilarious MAD LIBS® game!

MY LEAST FAVORITE NIGHT OF THE YEAR

EXCLAMATION _____

ANIMAL _____

PERSON IN ROOM _____

PART OF THE BODY _____

PART OF THE BODY (PLURAL) _____

PLURAL NOUN _____

NOUN _____

NUMBER _____

VERB _____

ADJECTIVE _____

TYPE OF LIQUID _____

ADJECTIVE _____

VERB ENDING IN "ING" _____

VERB _____

ADJECTIVE _____

MAD LIBS®
MY LEAST FAVORITE
NIGHT OF THE YEAR

_____! Is it New Year's Eve already? This is the worst night
EXCLAMATION

of the year for a pet _____ like me. Every other night of the
ANIMAL

year, I curl up with _____, who rubs my _____
PERSON IN ROOM   PART OF THE BODY

and scratches behind my _____. But on New Year's
PART OF THE BODY (PLURAL)

Eve, my life goes down the _____. Instead of snuggling up
PLURAL NOUN

on the _____ with my owner, I'm surrounded by _____
NOUN   NUMBER

humans who take over my home to party! They _____
VERB

their _____ noisemakers all night long. They spill
ADJECTIVE

_____ all over the floor, which makes my paws all
TYPE OF LIQUID

_____. Then suddenly, out of nowhere, they start shouting
ADJECTIVE

and _____ confetti! It's enough to make me want to
VERB ENDING IN "ING"

_____ away. I can't wait till this _____ night is over.
VERB   ADJECTIVE

MAD LIBS® is fun to play with friends, but you can also play it by yourself! To begin with, DO NOT look at the story on the page below. Fill in the blanks on this page with the words called for. Then, using the words you have selected, fill in the blank spaces in the story.

Now you've created your own hilarious MAD LIBS® game!

FIRST NIGHT FESTIVITIES

PLURAL NOUN _____

NUMBER _____

NOUN _____

ADJECTIVE _____

NOUN _____

PLURAL NOUN _____

ANIMAL (PLURAL) _____

TYPE OF FOOD (PLURAL) _____

ADJECTIVE _____

COLOR _____

CELEBRITY _____

ADJECTIVE _____

PLURAL NOUN _____

PLURAL NOUN _____

PLURAL NOUN _____

VEHICLE _____

TYPE OF FOOD (PLURAL) _____

ADJECTIVE _____

MAD LIBS

FIRST NIGHT FESTIVITIES

This New Year's Eve, bring your friends and _____ to First
PLURAL NOUN

Night—the one night a year when your hometown becomes a stage!

For only _____ dollars, you'll get an all-access _____ to
NUMBER   NOUN

all kinds of _____ events. There will be _____
ADJECTIVE   NOUN

jugglers, acrobats jumping through flaming _____, and
PLURAL NOUN

magicians making _____ pop out of their hats. Stop by
ANIMAL (PLURAL)

the First Night Petting Zoo, where there will be _____
TYPE OF FOOD (PLURAL)

to feed all the animals. Listen to _____ music from all around
ADJECTIVE

the world—from a folksy _____-grass trio to _____
COLOR   CELEBRITY

and the band the _____ _____. Make winter
ADJECTIVE   PLURAL NOUN

crafts out of _____ and _____ at the First
PLURAL NOUN   PLURAL NOUN

Night Craft Corner. With _____ rides, deep-fried
VEHICLE

_____, and _____ fireworks at midnight,
TYPE OF FOOD (PLURAL)   ADJECTIVE

there's something for everyone at First Night!

MAD LIBS® is fun to play with friends, but you can also play it by yourself! To begin with, DO NOT look at the story on the page below. Fill in the blanks on this page with the words called for. Then, using the words you have selected, fill in the blank spaces in the story.

Now you've created your own hilarious MAD LIBS® game!

NEW YEAR, NEW ROOM, NEW ME

ADJECTIVE _____

CELEBRITY _____

PLURAL NOUN _____

ADJECTIVE _____

COLOR _____

COLOR _____

ADJECTIVE _____

NOUN _____

ADJECTIVE _____

ADJECTIVE _____

CELEBRITY _____

PLURAL NOUN _____

NOUN _____

PERSON IN ROOM _____

ADJECTIVE _____

MAD LIBS®
NEW YEAR, NEW ROOM, NEW ME

I'm ready to make a big change to my _____ bedroom this
$\qquad$ ADJECTIVE

year. It's time to take down the _____ posters, clear off my
$\qquad$ CELEBRITY

shelves filled with _____ , and donate my _____
$\qquad$ PLURAL NOUN $\qquad$ ADJECTIVE

toys to charity. Those things represent the old me. The new me is all

about bright colors, like _____ and _____ ,
$\qquad$ COLOR $\qquad$ COLOR

and _____ vibes. The first thing I'm going to buy is
$\qquad$ ADJECTIVE

a/an _____ to hang from the ceiling. I'm getting a
$\qquad$ NOUN

new _____ bedspread and hanging a/an _____
$\qquad$ ADJECTIVE $\qquad$ ADJECTIVE

poster of _____ on my door. I'm filling my shelves with
$\qquad$ CELEBRITY

_____ . And I'm going to have the comfiest beanbag
PLURAL NOUN

_____ . I'm filling every space on my walls with framed
NOUN

pictures of my best friend, _____ . When you're hanging out
$\qquad$ PERSON IN ROOM

in my new room, you'll definitely feel _____ .
$\qquad$ ADJECTIVE

MAD LIBS® is fun to play with friends, but you can also play it by yourself! To begin with, DO NOT look at the story on the page below. Fill in the blanks on this page with the words called for. Then, using the words you have selected, fill in the blank spaces in the story.

Now you've created your own hilarious MAD LIBS® game!

NEW YEAR'S SWEET TREATS

PART OF THE BODY _____

NOUN _____

NOUN _____

TYPE OF FOOD _____

ADJECTIVE _____

NUMBER _____

PLURAL NOUN _____

NUMBER _____

NOUN _____

ADVERB _____

NUMBER _____

ADJECTIVE _____

PART OF THE BODY (PLURAL) _____

VERB _____

NOUN _____

MAD LIBS®

NEW YEAR'S SWEET TREATS

Try this _____-watering dessert for a sweet New Year's
     <u>PART OF THE BODY</u>
gathering.

Ingredients:

- 1 _____ cake mix
       <u>NOUN</u>

- 1 packet _____ pudding
               <u>NOUN</u>

- 1/2 cup _____ oil
             <u>TYPE OF FOOD</u>

- 1 cup _____ milk
           <u>ADJECTIVE</u>

- _____ ounces chocolate _____
     <u>NUMBER</u>   <u>PLURAL NOUN</u>

Directions:

Preheat oven to _____ degrees. In a/an _____ , combine
                   <u>NUMBER</u>   <u>NOUN</u>
cake mix with pudding. _____ stir in the oil and milk. Pour
                          <u>ADVERB</u>
batter into a pan and bake for _____ minutes or until cake is
                                  <u>NUMBER</u>
_____ . When cake is done, use your _____
   <u>ADJECTIVE</u>   <u>PART OF THE BODY (PLURAL)</u>
to mold the cake into balls. Melt the chocolate. Take the cake balls and

_____ them into the melted chocolate. Chill your chocolate
    <u>VERB</u>
cake balls in the _____ and be ready to munch on them at
                     <u>NOUN</u>
midnight!

MAD LIBS® is fun to play with friends, but you can also play it by yourself! To begin with, DO NOT look at the story on the page below. Fill in the blanks on this page with the words called for. Then, using the words you have selected, fill in the blank spaces in the story.

Now you've created your own hilarious MAD LIBS® game!

WORST NEW YEAR'S EVE EVER!

ADJECTIVE _____

COLOR _____

ARTICLE OF CLOTHING (PLURAL) _____

VERB ENDING IN "ING" _____

ANIMAL (PLURAL) _____

ARTICLE OF CLOTHING (PLURAL) _____

PERSON IN ROOM _____

NOUN _____

NUMBER _____

ADVERB _____

NUMBER _____

VERB (PAST TENSE) _____

ADJECTIVE _____

PART OF THE BODY _____

EXCLAMATION _____

ADJECTIVE _____

MAD LIBS®
WORST NEW YEAR'S EVE EVER!

This New Year's Eve, my _____ friends and I bought tickets
                            ADJECTIVE

to see our home team, the _____ _____,
                            COLOR   ARTICLE OF CLOTHING (PLURAL)

play against the _____ _____. We
                 VERB ENDING IN "ING"   ANIMAL (PLURAL)

heard they were giving out free team _____ at
                                      ARTICLE OF CLOTHING (PLURAL)

the game, and we just had to get some. Unfortunately, my friend

_____ lost our tickets. By the time I found the tickets
PERSON IN ROOM

hidden under the _____, we were _____ minutes late.
                  NOUN   NUMBER

When we finally got to the game, I ran _____ to the giveaway
                                       ADVERB

table—but all the free merchandise was gone! Oh well—at least I could

still catch the end of the game. The score was tied with _____
                                                          NUMBER

seconds left on the clock. Right before the buzzer, my team

_____ the ball and scored—right at midnight! The
VERB (PAST TENSE)

crowd went _____. It would have been great . . . if I hadn't
            ADJECTIVE

tripped on my shoelaces, hit my _____, and missed the
                                 PART OF THE BODY

whole thing. _____! I hope the rest of the year isn't as
              EXCLAMATION

_____ as this New Year's Eve.
ADJECTIVE

MAD LIBS® is fun to play with friends, but you can also play it by yourself! To begin with, DO NOT look at the story on the page below. Fill in the blanks on this page with the words called for. Then, using the words you have selected, fill in the blank spaces in the story.

Now you've created your own hilarious MAD LIBS® game!

BEST NEW YEAR'S EVE EVER!

ADJECTIVE _____

VERB ENDING IN "ING" _____

ADJECTIVE _____

PLURAL NOUN _____

CELEBRITY _____

PART OF THE BODY _____

NUMBER _____

TYPE OF FOOD _____

EXCLAMATION _____

PERSON IN ROOM _____

ADVERB _____

SAME CELEBRITY _____

SAME CELEBRITY _____

ANIMAL (PLURAL) _____

NOUN _____

ADJECTIVE _____

ADJECTIVE _____

ADJECTIVE _____

MAD LIBS®
BEST NEW YEAR'S EVE EVER!

What a/an _____ night! It was New Year's Eve and I was
             ADJECTIVE

_____ alone at home. I was so excited to watch my
VERB ENDING IN "ING"

favorite superhero movie, _____ *Woman vs. Space*
                          ADJECTIVE

_____ starring _____. Suddenly, something
PLURAL NOUN   CELEBRITY

caught my _____. I saw a gift card lying on the ground
          PART OF THE BODY

for _____ dollars to my favorite restaurant, the _____
    NUMBER   TYPE OF FOOD

Factory. _____! I called _____ and we
         EXCLAMATION   PERSON IN ROOM

_____ rushed over to the restaurant. And guess who was
ADVERB

waiting for a table? _____! I know everything about
                    SAME CELEBRITY

_____, so we talked about how we both have pet
SAME CELEBRITY

_____. Then I took out my _____ and we
ANIMAL (PLURAL)   NOUN

snapped a group photo. I said, "Happy _____ Year!" and
                                      ADJECTIVE

texted the photo to my mother, who's also a/an _____ fan.
                                               ADJECTIVE

This new year is already off to a/an _____ start!
                                    ADJECTIVE

MAD LIBS® is fun to play with friends, but you can also play it by yourself! To begin with, DO NOT look at the story on the page below. Fill in the blanks on this page with the words called for. Then, using the words you have selected, fill in the blank spaces in the story.

Now you've created your own hilarious MAD LIBS® game!

HOW TO STAY AWAKE UNTIL MIDNIGHT

PLURAL NOUN _____

ADJECTIVE _____

PART OF THE BODY (PLURAL) _____

ADJECTIVE _____

ADJECTIVE _____

VERB ENDING IN "ING" _____

TYPE OF FOOD (PLURAL) _____

PART OF THE BODY _____

TYPE OF LIQUID _____

PART OF THE BODY _____

NOUN _____

TYPE OF LIQUID _____

VERB ENDING IN "ING" _____

MAD LIBS
HOW TO STAY AWAKE
UNTIL MIDNIGHT

Staying awake until the stroke of midnight takes skill, endurance,

and _____ . Here are some _____ tips to keep
     PLURAL NOUN   ADJECTIVE

your _____ wide open until the new year:
    PART OF THE BODY (PLURAL)

- **DO** take _____ naps throughout the day so you'll be well
            ADJECTIVE

 rested for the night's festivities.

- **DON'T** listen to quiet music or a/an _____ podcast that
                            ADJECTIVE

 puts you to sleep.

- **DO** get your blood pumping by _____ around
                           VERB ENDING IN "ING"

 your house.

- **DON'T** eat too many _____ or you'll be sick to
                     TYPE OF FOOD (PLURAL)

 your _____ by midnight.
   PART OF THE BODY

- **DO** splash cold _____ on your _____ if
            TYPE OF LIQUID   PART OF THE BODY

 you're feeling sleepy.

- **DON'T** lie down on a comfortable _____ .
                               NOUN

- **DO** drink a lot of _____ . If you're _____
               TYPE OF LIQUID   VERB ENDING IN "ING"

 to the bathroom a lot, you're not falling asleep!

MAD LIBS® is fun to play with friends, but you can also play it by yourself! To begin with, DO NOT look at the story on the page below. Fill in the blanks on this page with the words called for. Then, using the words you have selected, fill in the blank spaces in the story.

Now you've created your own hilarious MAD LIBS® game!

MY NEW YEAR'S RESOLUTIONS

ADJECTIVE _____

ADJECTIVE _____

PLURAL NOUN _____

NUMBER _____

VERB _____

ADJECTIVE _____

VERB _____

TYPE OF FOOD _____

NOUN _____

TYPE OF FOOD _____

COLOR _____

COUNTRY _____

PLURAL NOUN _____

PERSON IN ROOM _____

A PLACE _____

NOUN _____

NUMBER _____

ANIMAL (PLURAL) _____

MAD LIBS®
MY NEW YEAR'S RESOLUTIONS

I have _____ plans for the new year! Every December, I make
         ADJECTIVE

a/an _____ list of all my resolutions. Here are just some of my
       ADJECTIVE

_____ for next year:
PLURAL NOUN

- Do _____ pull-ups and _____ -ups every day to get
       NUMBER   VERB

  strong

- Keep my room clean and _____ so my parents don't
                              ADJECTIVE

  _____ at me every week
      VERB

- Drink a healthy _____ smoothie every morning
                    TYPE OF FOOD

- Build the biggest _____ of all time
                        NOUN

- Make _____-flavored ice cream with red and
              TYPE OF FOOD

  _____ sprinkles
      COLOR

- Visit _____ to see the famous _____
            COUNTRY   PLURAL NOUN

- Take _____ to (the) _____ and buy them the
         PERSON IN ROOM   A PLACE

  shiniest _____ I can find
               NOUN

- Donate _____ dollars to save the endangered
             NUMBER

  _____
      ANIMAL (PLURAL)

MAD LIBS® is fun to play with friends, but you can also play it by yourself! To begin with, DO NOT look at the story on the page below. Fill in the blanks on this page with the words called for. Then, using the words you have selected, fill in the blank spaces in the story.

Now you've created your own hilarious MAD LIBS® game!

NEW YEAR'S DAY HOUR-BY-HOUR

PERSON IN ROOM _____

ADJECTIVE _____

PLURAL NOUN _____

PLURAL NOUN _____

PERSON IN ROOM _____

NUMBER _____

ADJECTIVE _____

TYPE OF FOOD _____

TYPE OF LIQUID _____

VERB _____

NOUN _____

NUMBER _____

NUMBER _____

CELEBRITY _____

VERB ENDING IN "ING" _____

MAD LIBS®
NEW YEAR'S DAY
HOUR-BY-HOUR

_____ once told me that how you spend New Year's Day is
PERSON IN ROOM

how you'll spend the whole year. If that's true, I've set myself up to have

the most _____ year ever!
ADJECTIVE

My schedule:

8 a.m.: Wake up and eat a bowl filled with my favorite cereals, Cocoa

_____ and Frosted _____
PLURAL NOUN   PLURAL NOUN

10 a.m.: Go to _____'s house and watch _____
PERSON IN ROOM   NUMBER

cartoons in a row

12 p.m.: Break for a/an _____ lunch of _____-burgers
ADJECTIVE   TYPE OF FOOD

and _____-shakes
TYPE OF LIQUID

2 p.m.: Go to the arcade to _____ some games. Win enough
VERB

tickets to buy a huge _____
NOUN

4 p.m.: On the way home, get ice cream with _____ toppings
NUMBER

6 p.m.: Have dinner and finish a/an _____-piece puzzle with
NUMBER

my family

8 p.m.: Have a dance party to music by _____
CELEBRITY

10 p.m.: Fall asleep while _____
VERB ENDING IN "ING"

From HAPPY NEW YEAR MAD LIBS® • Copyright © 2019 by Penguin Random House LLC.

MAD LIBS® is fun to play with friends, but you can also play it by yourself! To begin with, DO NOT look at the story on the page below. Fill in the blanks on this page with the words called for. Then, using the words you have selected, fill in the blank spaces in the story.

Now you've created your own hilarious MAD LIBS® game!

NEW YEAR'S ROCKIN' EVE

ADJECTIVE _____

VERB ENDING IN "ING" _____

FIRST NAME _____

VERB ENDING IN "S" _____

NUMBER _____

NOUN _____

ADJECTIVE _____

CELEBRITY _____

EXCLAMATION _____

PERSON IN ROOM _____

PART OF THE BODY _____

NOUN _____

OCCUPATION _____

ADJECTIVE _____

MAD☺LIBS®

NEW YEAR'S ROCKIN' EVE

Tonight's the _____ night! Welcome to the annual New Year's
ADJECTIVE

_____ Eve Countdown. I'm your host,
VERB ENDING IN "ING"

_____, broadcasting live from the city that never
FIRST NAME

_____. A record-breaking _____ people are
VERB ENDING IN "S"   NUMBER

here to watch the one-and-only famous _____ drop at
NOUN

midnight. But first, we have some _____ news to report from
ADJECTIVE

our main stage, where _____ is performing a live set.
CELEBRITY

_____! It appears that _____ is climbing onto
EXCLAMATION   PERSON IN ROOM

the stage. This person is now waving a/an _____ and singing
PART OF THE BODY

along to the hit song "You'll Always Be My _____." Uh-oh!
NOUN

Looks like a/an _____ is coming to end the party. I tell you,
OCCUPATION

folks, there is never a/an _____ moment on live TV!
ADJECTIVE

MAD LIBS® is fun to play with friends, but you can also play it by yourself! To begin with, DO NOT look at the story on the page below. Fill in the blanks on this page with the words called for. Then, using the words you have selected, fill in the blank spaces in the story.

Now you've created your own hilarious MAD LIBS® game!

THE FUTURE IS NOW

ADJECTIVE _____

VEHICLE _____

TYPE OF FOOD _____

ADJECTIVE _____

ADJECTIVE _____

NUMBER _____

FIRST NAME _____

NOUN _____

NOUN _____

EXCLAMATION _____

PLURAL NOUN _____

ADJECTIVE _____

VERB _____

MAD LIBS

THE FUTURE IS NOW

Kid 1: I can't wait for all the new and _____ gadgets that are
_____ADJECTIVE_____
coming out this year.

Kid 2: Me neither! I want to ride in a self-driving _____ .
_____VEHICLE_____
I heard they have _____ makers in them now. Yum!
_____TYPE OF FOOD_____

Kid 1: That sounds _____ . I want to try out one of those
_____ADJECTIVE_____
_____ virtual-reality headsets. I hear it's _____ times
___ADJECTIVE___   ___NUMBER___
cooler than actual reality.

Kid 2: I'm going to test out the new virtual assistant named

_____ . I'll make it call me "_____" instead
_____FIRST NAME_____   ___NOUN___
of my name.

Kid 1: That's so funny! Well, I'm going to test out the latest

_____ -vision goggles, so I can see in the dark.
___NOUN___

Kid 2: _____! Don't forget to check out those new
_____EXCLAMATION_____
pocket-size _____ . They look so cool.
____PLURAL NOUN____

Kid 1: Great idea! The future is going to be _____ .
_____ADJECTIVE_____

Kid 2: I know! I just want the future to hurry up and _____
_____VERB_____
here already.

From HAPPY NEW YEAR MAD LIBS® • Copyright © 2019 by Penguin Random House LLC.

MAD LIBS® is fun to play with friends, but you can also play it by yourself! To begin with, DO NOT look at the story on the page below. Fill in the blanks on this page with the words called for. Then, using the words you have selected, fill in the blank spaces in the story.

Now you've created your own hilarious MAD LIBS® game!

NEW YEAR'S BABY

FIRST NAME _____

SILLY WORD _____

NOUN _____

NUMBER _____

A PLACE _____

VERB _____

ADVERB _____

VEHICLE _____

NOUN _____

VERB (PAST TENSE) _____

ADJECTIVE _____

EXCLAMATION _____

NOUN _____

PART OF THE BODY (PLURAL) _____

ADJECTIVE _____

MAD LIBS

NEW YEAR'S BABY

Welcome to the world, Baby _____ —the very first baby
FIRST NAME

born this year! At _____ Hospital, this newborn bundle of
SILLY WORD

_____ arrived mere seconds after midnight, weighing in at
NOUN

_____ pounds. The parents were in (the) _____ when
NUMBER   A PLACE

they realized they needed to _____ to the hospital right away.
VERB

They raced there _____ , hoping the baby wouldn't be born in
ADVERB

the _____ . Luckily, they arrived just in the nick of
VEHICLE

_____ . When the baby was born, the doctors and nurses
NOUN

cheered and _____ . When the parents saw their
VERB (PAST TENSE)

_____ one for the first time, they cried out,
ADJECTIVE

" _____ !" "I can't believe how much our little
EXCLAMATION

_____ looks like me," said the new dad. "I don't know, dear,
NOUN

those are definitely my _____ ," the new mom said
PART OF THE BODY (PLURAL)

proudly. For this new family of three, it was truly a/an _____
ADJECTIVE

new year!

MAD LIBS® is fun to play with friends, but you can also play it by yourself! To begin with, DO NOT look at the story on the page below. Fill in the blanks on this page with the words called for. Then, using the words you have selected, fill in the blank spaces in the story.

Now you've created your own hilarious MAD LIBS® game!

NEW YEAR HOROSCOPES, PART 1

VERB _____

ARTICLE OF CLOTHING (PLURAL) _____

VERB _____

VERB _____

OCCUPATION (PLURAL) _____

ADJECTIVE _____

VERB _____

ADJECTIVE _____

NOUN _____

ADJECTIVE _____

ADJECTIVE _____

VERB _____

ADJECTIVE _____

NOUN _____

ANIMAL _____

ADJECTIVE _____

Nobody knows what the future will _____ . Here's what the
<u>VERB</u>

stars predict for the new year:

Aries (Mar. 21–Apr. 19): Hold on to your _____!
<u>ARTICLE OF CLOTHING (PLURAL)</u>

This year is going to _____ . Embrace your new motto: If I
<u>VERB</u>

can dream it, I can _____ it.
<u>VERB</u>

Taurus (Apr. 20–May 20): People with your sign often grow up to be

_____ . Embrace your _____ skills and you'll
<u>OCCUPATION (PLURAL)</u>   <u>ADJECTIVE</u>

go far.

Gemini (May 21–June 20): You can never _____ still, and this
<u>VERB</u>

year is no different. Take _____ trips to explore new places!
<u>ADJECTIVE</u>

Cancer (June 21–July 22): Friends and family mean the _____
<u>NOUN</u>

to you. Make them feel _____ and you'll feel _____ , too.
<u>ADJECTIVE</u>   <u>ADJECTIVE</u>

Leo (July 23–Aug. 22): For someone who loves to _____ for
<u>VERB</u>

an audience, this year will be _____ . You'll shine like a/an
<u>ADJECTIVE</u>

_____ .
<u>NOUN</u>

Virgo (Aug. 23–Sept. 22): Attack new challenges like a/an _____
<u>ANIMAL</u>

attacks its prey. Be bold and your year will be _____ .
<u>ADJECTIVE</u>

MAD LIBS® is fun to play with friends, but you can also play it by yourself! To begin with, DO NOT look at the story on the page below. Fill in the blanks on this page with the words called for. Then, using the words you have selected, fill in the blank spaces in the story.

Now you've created your own hilarious MAD LIBS® game!

NEW YEAR HOROSCOPES, PART 2

ADJECTIVE _____

PART OF THE BODY _____

ADJECTIVE _____

ARTICLE OF CLOTHING (PLURAL) _____

VERB _____

ADJECTIVE _____

ADJECTIVE _____

VERB _____

PART OF THE BODY _____

TYPE OF LIQUID _____

VERB _____

VERB _____

PART OF THE BODY _____

VERB ENDING IN "ING" _____

Check out these _____ horoscopes for the year ahead:
ADJECTIVE

Libra (Sept. 23–Oct. 22): Beauty is in the _____ of the
PART OF THE BODY

beholder. Let's get you feeling _____ with some new
ADJECTIVE

_____ to rock your look.
ARTICLE OF CLOTHING (PLURAL)

Scorpio (Oct. 23–Nov. 21): Petty drama will _____ you in
VERB

the new year. Remember, when they go low, you go _____ .
ADJECTIVE

Sagittarius (Nov. 22–Dec. 21): This is the _____ year for a
ADJECTIVE

new hobby. If you've always wanted to _____ , this is the
VERB

time to do it!

Capricorn (Dec. 22–Jan. 19): Your year starts off on the wrong

_____ . But when life gives you lemons, make
PART OF THE BODY

_____ !
TYPE OF LIQUID

Aquarius (Jan. 20–Feb. 18): You were born to _____ problems,
VERB

water child. Help others who can't _____ themselves.
VERB

Pisces (Feb. 19–Mar. 20): Get your _____ out of the
PART OF THE BODY

clouds this year. Stay grounded by _____ with good
VERB ENDING IN "ING"

friends as much as possible.

MAD LIBS® is fun to play with friends, but you can also play it by yourself! To begin with, DO NOT look at the story on the page below. Fill in the blanks on this page with the words called for. Then, using the words you have selected, fill in the blank spaces in the story.

Now you've created your own hilarious MAD LIBS® game!

HISTORY OF THE FIRST NEW YEAR

NUMBER _____

PLURAL NOUN _____

FIRST NAME _____

VERB ENDING IN "ING" _____

OCCUPATION (PLURAL) _____

PERSON IN ROOM _____

ADJECTIVE _____

PART OF THE BODY (PLURAL) _____

VERB _____

VERB _____

ADVERB _____

PLURAL NOUN _____

PLURAL NOUN _____

PLURAL NOUN _____

ADJECTIVE _____

TYPE OF FOOD (PLURAL) _____

TYPE OF LIQUID _____

HISTORY OF THE FIRST NEW YEAR

The calendar year hasn't always been _____ months long. In
NUMBER

ancient times, there were only ten _____ in a year. The
PLURAL NOUN

Roman emperor _____ Caesar added two months to the
FIRST NAME

calendar after _____ with the smartest astronomers
VERB ENDING IN "ING"

and _____. The new first month of the year was
OCCUPATION (PLURAL)

named after _____, the Roman god of beginnings. This
PERSON IN ROOM

_____ god was thought to have two _____:
ADJECTIVE   PART OF THE BODY (PLURAL)

one that could _____ into the past and one that could
VERB

_____ into the future. Caesar _____ declared
VERB   ADVERB

January 1 as the first day of the new year. Roman citizens celebrated

by offering _____ to the gods, giving _____ as
PLURAL NOUN   PLURAL NOUN

gifts, and decorating their homes with _____. They
PLURAL NOUN

threw _____ parties with lots of food and drink. Fast-forward
ADJECTIVE

to today and we're still celebrating the same way—with lots of

_____ and _____!
TYPE OF FOOD (PLURAL)   TYPE OF LIQUID

MAD LIBS® is fun to play with friends, but you can also play it by yourself! To begin with, DO NOT look at the story on the page below. Fill in the blanks on this page with the words called for. Then, using the words you have selected, fill in the blank spaces in the story.

Now you've created your own hilarious MAD LIBS® game!

MY TOAST TO THE NEW YEAR

PLURAL NOUN _____

ADJECTIVE _____

VERB _____

TYPE OF LIQUID _____

VERB _____

PLURAL NOUN _____

TYPE OF FOOD (PLURAL) _____

TYPE OF FOOD (PLURAL) _____

EXCLAMATION _____

ADJECTIVE _____

ADJECTIVE _____

SILLY WORD _____

MY TOAST TO THE NEW YEAR

Family, friends, and _____ —I'm so _____ that
              PLURAL NOUN   ADJECTIVE

we're all here together to _____ the new year. Let's raise a
                                  VERB

glass of _____ and toast to the future. May we get to
         TYPE OF LIQUID

_____ our friends and families who live near and far. May
   VERB

we have enough _____ to share with our loved ones. May
                 PLURAL NOUN

we have lots of _____ and _____
                TYPE OF FOOD (PLURAL)   TYPE OF FOOD (PLURAL)

for our dinner tables. Now wave goodbye to the past and say

" _____ " to the _____ future. Out with the old
   EXCLAMATION   ADJECTIVE

and in with the _____ . Let's say cheers, and toast to a/an
                 ADJECTIVE

_____ new year!
  SILLY WORD